Paris Fury

Paris Fury: A Tale of Love, Strength, and Family

Paris Fury, born as Paris Mulroy in 1989, is a name that resonates with resilience, love, and family values. Hailing from Doncaster, South Yorkshire, England, she was raised in a traditional gypsy family, an upbringing that undoubtedly influenced her strong bond with family and her unwavering support for her husband, the famed heavyweight boxer Tyson Fury.

Despite facing challenges from a young age, Paris managed to complete her high school education before stepping into the role of a devoted homemaker and mother. Her journey into adulthood took an unexpected turn when she met Tyson Fury, then a rising boxing star, at a mutual friend's wedding when she was just 15 years old. Destiny played its part, reuniting them on Paris's 16th birthday, and thus began a love story that would withstand the tests of time and trials.

Their love story culminated in a beautiful traditional wedding in 2008, witnessed by over 300 guests in Paris's hometown. Since then, Paris and Tyson have stood together through thick and thin, carving out a life that's a testament to their love and devotion. Their union has brought forth a brood of six children, each adding a new layer of joy, chaos, and love to their already vibrant family.

Paris's role as a homemaker and mother has been her most significant endeavor. She has been the rock that anchors the Fury family, supporting her husband through his highs and lows, including his remarkable victories in the boxing ring. One memorable instance was her spirited presence at the Tyson Fury vs. Deontay Wilder fight, where she cheered tirelessly for her husband, celebrating his triumph in the seventh round.

Paris's life isn't just confined to the domestic sphere. She has also managed to shine as an internet sensation, amassing a substantial following on her social media platforms, with over a million followers on Instagram and nearly 50,000 on Twitter. Her popularity is a testament to her charm, relatability, and strength as a woman who embraces her role while maintaining her individuality.

In 2021, Paris added the title of an author to her repertoire with the release of her book, "Love and Fury: The Magic and Mayhem of Life with Tyson." This intimate memoir gives readers a glimpse into the behind-the-scenes moments of their relationship, painting a vivid picture of the challenges they've faced and the love that has carried them through.

Paris's journey hasn't been without its share of trials. She endured the heartache of two miscarriages, a painful chapter that further cemented the importance of family and the strength it takes to overcome adversity.

As Paris continues to inspire her followers with her unwavering love for her family, her endearing bond with her husband, and her unapologetic individuality, one thing remains clear: Paris Fury is more than just the wife of a heavyweight boxer. She's a symbol of love, strength, and resilience, and her story is a testament to the power of family, dedication, and the beauty of embracing life's challenges with open arms.

An Adventurous Life Fueled by Love and Determination

Paris Fury's life is a remarkable journey that has been intertwined with her husband Tyson Fury's meteoric rise in the world of boxing. While Tyson's fame and success have grown, Paris has remained his steadfast anchor and the heart of their family.

Paris's blonde hair and hazel blue eyes exude an aura of warmth and approachability, traits that have endeared her to fans and followers around the world. Standing at 5 feet 4 inches tall, she may be shorter than her towering husband, but her presence is larger than life. Her hourglass figure and vibrant smile reflect the joy she finds in her roles as a wife, mother, and self-made personality.

Born into a traditional gypsy family in Doncaster, South Yorkshire, Paris's upbringing instilled in her the values of family, loyalty, and community. She shares a special bond with her sister, Lynda Mulroy, and often showcases their close relationship on social media. Though Paris's formal education was cut short due to familial responsibilities, she has embraced her role as a mother with grace and determination, putting her family's needs at the forefront.

As a homemaker, Paris has not only nurtured her children but also become a beacon of strength for Tyson Fury. While Tyson's boxing career has been marked by triumphs, including becoming the third heavyweight in history to hold The Ring Journal Championship twice, it hasn't been without its challenges. Paris's unwavering support has been crucial during Tyson's battles both in and out of the ring, making her an integral part of his journey.

Despite being focused on her family, Paris has managed to carve out her own identity as a social media influencer. With over a million followers on Instagram and a significant presence on Twitter, she connects with fans on a personal level, offering glimpses into her life, thoughts, and the moments that matter most to her. Her authenticity and relatability have garnered her a dedicated following who admire her as not just a celebrity spouse, but as a woman of substance.

In 2021, Paris took her story beyond social media by publishing her book, "Love and Fury: The Magic and Mayhem of Life with Tyson." This candid memoir gives readers a peek behind the curtains, shedding light on the challenges, triumphs, and love that have defined her relationship with Tyson. Through the pages of her book, Paris invites readers into her world, sharing the complexities of balancing love, family, and fame.

Paris Fury's life is a testament to the power of love, determination, and embracing the unexpected twists that life presents. From her early days as a young gypsy girl to her role as a beloved wife, mother, and social media influencer, Paris continues to captivate hearts with her authenticity and strength. Her story is a reminder that behind every great man stands an equally remarkable woman, and Paris Fury's journey is an inspiring tale of love, resilience, and the magic of an adventurous life well-lived.

Love that Defied Odds: Paris Fury's Extraordinary Journey

Paris Fury's life is a tapestry woven with threads of love, perseverance, and the unwavering commitment that she shares with her husband, Tyson Fury. Born as Paris Mulroy in 1989, she hails from the picturesque town of Doncaster in South Yorkshire, England. Raised in a traditional gypsy family, Paris's formative years were imbued with values of family unity, loyalty, and the profound importance of standing by one another through thick and thin.

Educated at her local high school, Paris's life took an unexpected turn when she crossed paths with a young and rising boxer named Tyson Fury. Destiny seemed to play a hand as their initial meeting at a friend's wedding led to a serendipitous reunion on Paris's 16th birthday. Little did they know that this seemingly ordinary encounter would evolve into an extraordinary love story that would stand the test of time.

Their love story culminated in a fairytale wedding on November 8, 2008, in Paris's hometown. The ceremony, steeped in tradition and attended by more than 300 guests, marked the beginning of a journey that would be marked by challenges, triumphs, and an unbreakable bond.

In a world where fame often comes at the cost of stability, Paris Fury has managed to strike a unique balance between her role as a homemaker and her status as a social media sensation. As a mother of six children, she has embraced her responsibilities with grace and dedication, forming the cornerstone of her family's foundation. Her resilience and nurturing spirit have not only endeared her to her husband and children but have also resonated with her ever-growing fan base.

Paris's presence on social media platforms, particularly Instagram and Twitter, showcases her authenticity and charm. With over a million followers on Instagram and nearly 50,000 on Twitter, she engages with her audience on a personal level, offering a glimpse into her life, thoughts, and the joys of motherhood. Her relatability has transformed her from a celebrity spouse to a role model for many who admire her strength and individuality.

Paris Fury's journey extends beyond her roles as a wife and mother. In 2021, she added the title of author to her repertoire with the release of her book, "Love and Fury: The Magic and Mayhem of Life with Tyson." This intimate memoir provides an insider's view into the ups and downs of their relationship, offering readers a glimpse into the life behind the headlines and the sacrifices made for love.

Paris's life is not without its share of challenges. She has experienced the heartache of two miscarriages, a painful reminder of life's fragility. Through these trials, she has displayed an immense capacity for resilience and an unyielding devotion to her family.

Paris Fury's story is a testament to the power of love, faith, and perseverance. Her journey from a traditional gypsy upbringing to becoming the wife of a heavyweight boxing champion is a testament to her ability to navigate life's unpredictable paths with grace and determination. As she continues to inspire and uplift through her presence, both online and in the lives of her loved ones, Paris Fury remains a symbol of love's endurance, the strength of family, and the magic of a life lived with unwavering devotion.

A Life of Love and Resilience: Paris Fury's Enduring Legacy

Paris Fury's life story is one that radiates love, resilience, and the power of a strong partnership. Born as Paris Mulroy in 1989 in the charming town of Doncaster, South Yorkshire, England, she grew up in the embrace of a traditional gypsy family, instilling in her the core values of loyalty, family, and unwavering support.

Paris's journey took an unexpected turn when she crossed paths with a young and aspiring boxer, Tyson Fury. Their initial meeting at a friend's wedding seemed ordinary, but fate had grander plans. A chance reunion on Paris's 16th birthday sparked a love story that would evolve into an unbreakable bond. Their union was sealed in a fairytale wedding in 2008, witnessed by hundreds of guests in Paris's hometown.

Throughout their journey, Paris remained a constant pillar of strength for Tyson, standing by his side as he carved a name for himself in the boxing world. While her husband's career soared to remarkable heights, Paris embraced her role as a homemaker with grace and dedication. The heart of her family, she lovingly nurtured their six children and provided the foundation upon which their extraordinary life was built.

In addition to her role within her family, Paris's genuine charm and relatability captured the hearts of an ever-growing audience on social media. With over a million followers on Instagram and tens of thousands on Twitter, she has become an internet sensation in her own right. Her online presence offers a candid glimpse into her life, showcasing the everyday moments that make her a role model for many.

Paris's influence extended even further with the release of her book, "Love and Fury: The Magic and Mayhem of Life with Tyson," in 2021. This deeply personal memoir unveiled the untold stories behind the headlines, sharing the highs, lows, and sacrifices that define their journey together. It is a testament to their enduring love and the strength of their partnership.

The journey hasn't been without challenges. Paris bravely navigated the heartbreak of two miscarriages, a testament to her resilience and her ability to find strength in the face of adversity. Her openness about these struggles has resonated with countless women, reinforcing the idea that vulnerability can be a source of empowerment.

Paris Fury's life story is a canvas painted with love, determination, and an unyielding commitment to family. From her traditional gypsy roots to her role as the wife of a heavyweight champion, she has evolved into a symbol of inspiration for people around the world. Her enduring legacy lies not only in her unwavering support for Tyson but also in her ability to stand tall in her own right, embracing every facet of her identity with grace and authenticity.

As she continues to navigate life's twists and turns, Paris Fury remains a beacon of love, resilience, and the power of a strong partnership. Her journey is a testament to the idea that love, when nurtured with care, can weather any storm and create a legacy that inspires generations to come.

Love's Triumph: The Paris Fury Story

Paris Fury's life story is a remarkable tapestry woven with threads of love, strength, and an unwavering commitment to family. Born Paris Mulroy in 1989 in the quaint town of Doncaster, South Yorkshire, England, her early years were steeped in the values of her traditional gypsy heritage. These roots would later shape her unbreakable bond with her husband, the renowned heavyweight boxer Tyson Fury.

The story of Paris and Tyson is a testament to destiny's hand at work. Their paths first crossed at a friend's wedding, a seemingly ordinary encounter that would later lead to a fateful reunion on Paris's 16th birthday. From that moment, their lives became intertwined, embarking on a journey that would see them overcome challenges, celebrate victories, and build an unshakeable partnership.

In 2008, the world witnessed the culmination of their love story as they exchanged vows in a magical wedding attended by over 300 guests in Paris's hometown. This marked the beginning of their life together, a life that would be defined by their unyielding commitment to one another.

As the wife of a prominent athlete, Paris's role goes beyond the conventional. She is the heart and soul of their family, a pillar of strength supporting Tyson's meteoric rise in the boxing world. Through victories and setbacks, Paris has remained a steadfast source of encouragement, a testament to the power of love in the face of adversity.

Beyond her role as a loving wife, Paris has embraced the digital age with her presence on social media platforms. With more than a million followers on Instagram and a substantial following on Twitter, she has used her platform to share glimpses of her life, providing fans with a front-row seat to her journey. Her authenticity and relatability have transformed her into an inspiration for individuals seeking to find strength and beauty in their own lives.

In 2021, Paris added "author" to her list of accomplishments with the release of her book, "Love and Fury: The Magic and Mayhem of Life with Tyson." This candid memoir offers an intimate look into the challenges and joys of their relationship, shedding light on the sacrifices and triumphs that define their love story.

Despite her share of hardships, including the heartache of two miscarriages, Paris's spirit remains unbreakable. Her ability to weather storms with grace and resilience is a testament to her character and the unshakable bond she shares with Tyson and their family.

Paris Fury's journey is a tale of love that defies odds and triumphs over obstacles. From her traditional gypsy upbringing to her role as a strong and influential figure, she continues to inspire with her unwavering dedication to family, her vibrant presence on social media, and her resilience in the face of challenges. As she navigates life's unpredictable terrain, Paris Fury remains a beacon of love, strength, and the enduring power of a united heart.

Paris Fury: An Unbreakable Love

Paris Fury's life story is an embodiment of love, resilience, and the strength of the human spirit. Born Paris Mulroy in 1989, in the picturesque town of Doncaster, South Yorkshire, England, she grew up surrounded by the rich tapestry of her traditional gypsy heritage. Little did she know that her life would intertwine with that of a rising boxing star, Tyson Fury, leading to a love story that would capture hearts around the world.

Their journey began with a serendipitous encounter at a friend's wedding, but fate had more in store for them. A chance reunion on Paris's 16th birthday ignited a spark that would grow into an unbreakable bond. Their love story unfolded with a fairytale wedding in 2008, witnessed by hundreds of well-wishers in Paris's hometown. From that day forward, their lives became a testament to the power of love, unity, and mutual support.

While Tyson Fury's boxing career reached dazzling heights, Paris remained a steady anchor, providing unwavering support through every victory and challenge. As a mother of six children, she embraced her role as the heart of their family, nurturing their children with love and devotion. Her strong presence and nurturing spirit have made her a guiding force in the Fury household, a testament to the importance of family bonds.

In the age of social media, Paris has harnessed her influence to connect with a wider audience. Her online presence, boasting over a million followers on Instagram and a substantial following on Twitter, offers an authentic and relatable window into her life. Beyond being the wife of a celebrity, Paris is a role model for many, celebrated for her strength, grace, and down-to-earth personality.

Paris's journey took an even more profound turn with the release of her book, "Love and Fury: The Magic and Mayhem of Life with Tyson," published in 2021. This candid memoir delves into the intimate moments and challenges that have shaped their relationship, revealing the complex layers of their enduring love.

Throughout her life, Paris has shown remarkable strength in the face of adversity. Her openness about the pain of two miscarriages serves as a testament to her resilience and courage. Even in the midst of hardship, she remains an unwavering pillar of support for her family, a beacon of strength for her children, and an inspiration to countless admirers.

As she navigates the ever-changing tides of life, Paris Fury continues to shine as a symbol of love's unbreakable bonds, the triumph of the human spirit, and the beauty of embracing every facet of one's journey. Her story is a testament to the transformative power of love, the strength of family, and the resounding impact of living life with unwavering dedication.

Paris Fury: A Life Woven with Love and Purpose

Paris Fury's life is a remarkable journey that weaves together threads of love, resilience, and purpose. Born as Paris Mulroy in 1989 in the charming town of Doncaster, South Yorkshire, England, her story would soon become one of inspiration and unbreakable bonds.

Paris's path took an unexpected turn when she crossed paths with a young boxer named Tyson Fury. Their first meeting at a friend's wedding would set the stage for a fateful reunion on Paris's 16th birthday, igniting a love story that would weather the tests of time and trials. Their union was solidified in a breathtaking wedding ceremony in 2008, witnessed by a community of family and friends.

As Tyson Fury's boxing career ascended to new heights, Paris stood by his side as a pillar of strength. She embraced her role as a homemaker with unwavering dedication, nurturing their six children and creating a warm and loving home environment. Her resilience and fortitude shine as she balances her responsibilities with her presence on social media, where she has amassed a following of over a million on Instagram and a substantial audience on Twitter.

Paris's journey took a new direction with the release of her book, "Love and Fury: The Magic and Mayhem of Life with Tyson," in 2021. In this candid memoir, she offers readers an intimate look into the intricacies of their relationship, revealing the challenges, triumphs, and deep bond that have carried them through the years.

Amid life's joys, Paris has faced her share of heartache, including the pain of two miscarriages. Her openness about these experiences showcases her strength and vulnerability, touching the hearts of many who find solace in her words.

Paris Fury's story is one of a woman who embraces every facet of her life with authenticity and purpose. Her enduring love for Tyson, her role as a devoted mother, and her presence as a relatable figure in the digital world all come together to create a narrative of empowerment and inspiration. Her life embodies the beauty of standing strong in the face of challenges, cherishing love, and finding strength in unity.

As Paris continues to navigate her journey, her legacy remains one of love's triumph over adversity, the power of family bonds, and the impact of embracing life's unpredictability with grace and determination. Her story is a beacon of hope, reminding us all that life's most beautiful moments often arise from the tapestry of ordinary days woven with threads of love.

Paris Fury's life is a compelling narrative of love, courage, and unwavering devotion. Born Paris Mulroy in 1989 in the picturesque town of Doncaster, South Yorkshire, England, she embarked on a journey that would lead her to become not only the beloved wife of heavyweight boxer Tyson Fury but also a symbol of strength and resilience.

From the outset, Paris's life was colored by the rich tapestry of her traditional gypsy heritage. This background instilled in her the values of family unity, loyalty, and the importance of standing strong in the face of adversity. These values would later shape her role as a wife, mother, and source of inspiration to countless admirers.

Paris's story took an extraordinary turn when she met Tyson Fury. Their chance encounter at a friend's wedding paved the way for a serendipitous reunion on Paris's 16th birthday. This fateful meeting marked the beginning of a love story that would capture hearts worldwide. In 2008, their love culminated in a captivating wedding ceremony, witnessed by a community of family and friends.

Throughout Tyson Fury's storied boxing career, Paris remained his constant support, proving herself to be a true cornerstone of their family. As a mother of six children, she embraced her role with grace, nurturing their children with love, guidance, and an unbreakable bond. Her strength and resilience shone through as she managed her family responsibilities while sharing her life's journey on social media.

With over a million followers on Instagram and a substantial presence on Twitter, Paris leveraged her platform to connect with fans on a personal level. Her authenticity and relatability transformed her into more than just a celebrity spouse; she became a beacon of inspiration for individuals seeking to find strength, purpose, and beauty in their own lives.

In 2021, Paris added "author" to her list of accomplishments with the release of her book, "Love and Fury: The Magic and Mayhem of Life with Tyson." This poignant memoir offers an intimate look into their relationship, revealing the challenges, triumphs, and the profound love that have sustained them through the years.

Paris's journey has been marked by both triumphs and heartaches. Her openness about the pain of two miscarriages illustrates her resilience and her ability to turn challenges into opportunities for growth. Through it all, she remains an unwavering source of strength for her family and an inspiration to all who follow her journey.

Paris Fury's life story is a testament to the transformative power of love, the strength that comes from embracing one's true self, and the courage to stand tall in the face of life's uncertainties. As she continues to navigate life's twists and turns, Paris's legacy shines brightly as a beacon of love's enduring power, the importance of family bonds, and the impact of a life lived authentically and with purpose.

Paris Fury: A Trailblazer of Love and Empowerment

The life of Paris Fury is a compelling narrative that encapsulates love, empowerment, and an unyielding spirit. Born as Paris Mulroy in 1989 in the charming town of Doncaster, South Yorkshire, England, her journey is one that defies norms and inspires countless individuals around the world.

From her early years, Paris was steeped in the traditions of her traditional gypsy heritage, learning the values of family unity, resilience, and unwavering commitment. These values would shape the remarkable path she was destined to take.

Paris's destiny took a remarkable turn when she crossed paths with Tyson Fury, a young boxer with dreams of greatness. Their initial encounter at a friend's wedding set the stage for a serendipitous reunion on Paris's 16th birthday, sparking a love story that would resonate far beyond their immediate circle. Their union was solidified in a wedding ceremony in 2008 that captured the hearts of everyone who witnessed it.

As Tyson Fury's boxing career soared to new heights, Paris stood steadfastly by his side, becoming an unwavering source of support and strength. While nurturing their six children and cultivating a loving home environment, she also ventured into the world of social media. With over a million followers on Instagram and a significant presence on Twitter, she used her platform to share her authentic self and empower others to embrace their own uniqueness.

In 2021, Paris's story took on a new dimension with the release of her book, "Love and Fury: The Magic and Mayhem of Life with Tyson." This memoir offers an intimate and candid look into their relationship, revealing the challenges, the moments of joy, and the depth of their unwavering love

Despite her share of heartaches, including the pain of two miscarriages, Paris's spirit remains unbreakable. Her willingness to openly share her experiences has touched the lives of countless individuals who find solace in her resilience and courage.

Paris Fury's journey is a testament to the power of love, authenticity, and the strength to overcome adversity. Beyond being the wife of a boxing champion, she is a trailblazer who champions empowerment and self-love. Her legacy resonates as a beacon of inspiration for those navigating their own paths, reminding us all that true strength is found in embracing our individuality, weathering life's storms, and forging a legacy of love and empowerment.

The life story of Paris Fury is an embodiment of love, strength, and a profound impact that reaches far beyond the boxing ring. Born as Paris Mulroy in 1989 in the charming town of Doncaster, South Yorkshire, England, her journey through life has been marked by resilience, devotion, and a deep-seated commitment to family.

From her formative years within a traditional gypsy family, Paris imbibed values of unity, loyalty, and unwavering support. These values would later become the cornerstones of her identity as a wife, mother, and advocate for empowerment.

Paris's life took an extraordinary turn when she crossed paths with Tyson Fury. Their initial meeting at a friend's wedding set the stage for a serendipitous reconnection on Paris's 16th birthday, igniting a love story that would transcend time and challenge. Their union was solidified in a captivating wedding ceremony in 2008, a celebration of their love witnessed by a community of friends and family.

Throughout Tyson Fury's illustrious boxing career, Paris remained his unwavering source of strength. As a mother to six children, she embraced her role with grace and dedication, nurturing their family with love and compassion. Amid her family responsibilities, she also found her voice on social media, amassing over a million followers on Instagram and a significant presence on Twitter. Through these platforms, she inspires others to embrace their individuality and celebrate their journeys.

In 2021, Paris's story gained a new chapter with the release of her book, "Love and Fury: The Magic and Mayhem of Life with Tyson." This poignant memoir offers readers an intimate glimpse into their relationship, sharing the highs, the lows, and the profound love that has carried them through the years.

Through moments of triumph and adversity, Paris's strength shines brightly. Her willingness to openly discuss the pain of two miscarriages showcases her vulnerability and resilience, making her a relatable figure for countless individuals who have faced similar challenges.

Paris Fury's life is a legacy of love that transcends boundaries and touches hearts. Beyond being the wife of a renowned boxer, she is a symbol of empowerment and authenticity. Her journey reminds us all that strength is found in embracing our uniqueness, weathering life's storms with grace, and leaving a lasting impact through acts of kindness and unwavering love.

As Paris continues to navigate life's twists and turns, her legacy endures as a source of inspiration, reminding us that our lives are shaped not only by our accomplishments but by the love and connections we nurture along the way. Her story is a testament to the transformative power of love, the resilience of the human spirit, and the profound influence one individual can have on the lives of many.

Paris Fury: Embracing Love and Empowerment

The life journey of Paris Fury is a tapestry of love, empowerment, and unyielding strength. Born as Paris Mulroy in 1989 in the enchanting town of Doncaster, South Yorkshire, England, her path has been a testament to resilience, devotion, and a commitment to making a positive impact.

Paris's early years were shaped by her traditional gypsy heritage, instilling in her the values of family unity, loyalty, and the importance of standing by one another. These values laid the foundation for the remarkable journey that awaited her.

A chance meeting at a friend's wedding and a serendipitous reunion on Paris's 16th birthday led her to Tyson Fury, a rising star in the world of boxing. Their love story blossomed and flourished, culminating in a captivating wedding ceremony in 2008, a celebration of their deep bond witnessed by a community of loved ones.

As Tyson Fury's boxing career soared to new heights, Paris stood as his steadfast pillar of support. Amid nurturing their six children and creating a warm family environment, she found her voice on social media. With over a million followers on Instagram and a significant presence on Twitter, Paris used her platform to inspire, empower, and connect with her audience.

In 2021, Paris's story took a poignant turn with the release of her book, "Love and Fury: The Magic and Mayhem of Life with Tyson." In this intimate memoir, she opens up about the complexities of their relationship, revealing the challenges, joys, and unwavering love that have defined their journey.

Even in the face of adversity, including the pain of two miscarriages, Paris's spirit remains unbreakable. Her candidness about these experiences resonates deeply with others who find solace in her courage and resilience.

Paris Fury's life is a testament to the transformative power of love and authenticity. Beyond being the wife of a boxing champion, she is a beacon of empowerment, encouraging others to embrace their true selves and navigate life's challenges with grace. Her legacy is one of love, empowerment, and making a difference in the lives of those she touches.

As Paris continues to chart her course through life's unpredictable currents, her story reminds us that our impact is measured not just by our achievements, but by the love, support, and inspiration we bring to others. Her journey exemplifies the strength of the human spirit and the enduring power of love to overcome adversity and create a legacy of empowerment.

Paris Fury's life is a symphony of love, resilience, and the indomitable spirit that shapes her journey. Born Paris Mulroy in 1989 in the idyllic town of Doncaster, South Yorkshire, England, her life's narrative weaves together the threads of love, family, and unwavering strength.

Paris's early years were enriched by her traditional gypsy heritage, a foundation that instilled in her the values of unity, loyalty, and standing strong in the face of challenges. These values became the bedrock of her identity as she embarked on a path that would change her life forever.

The chance encounter at a friend's wedding and the serendipitous reunion on Paris's 16th birthday introduced her to Tyson Fury, a burgeoning boxing sensation. Their love story unfolded with a richness that would surpass imagination, culminating in a captivating wedding ceremony in 2008, witnessed by a host of friends and family.

As Tyson Fury's boxing career reached meteoric heights, Paris stood as an unwavering source of support. Amid the joys and responsibilities of raising their six children, she found her voice on social media. With over a million followers on Instagram and a significant presence on Twitter, Paris utilized her platform to inspire, connect, and empower individuals from all walks of life.

In 2021, Paris's narrative deepened with the release of her book, "Love and Fury: The Magic and Mayhem of Life with Tyson." This intimate memoir illuminated the complexities of their relationship, revealing the depth of their love and the resilience that sustains them through life's trials.

Even in the face of adversity, such as the heartache of two miscarriages, Paris's spirit remains unbreakable. Her candor in sharing these experiences has touched countless lives, providing solace and inspiration to those who have faced similar challenges.

Paris Fury's life embodies the essence of love's transformative power and the strength that comes from embracing one's true self. Beyond her role as the wife of a boxing champion, she is an emblem of empowerment, encouraging individuals to embrace their individuality and rise above life's hurdles. Her legacy is etched in the hearts of those who have been inspired by her story.

As Paris forges ahead, her journey continues to remind us that our impact goes beyond our accomplishments. It is defined by the love we share, the authenticity we embrace, and the inspiration we ignite in others. Her story is a testament to the human spirit's capacity to overcome challenges, foster connections, and leave a lasting legacy of love, strength, and empowerment.

The life story of Paris Fury is a masterpiece woven with threads of love, courage, and empowerment. Born as Paris Mulroy in 1989 in the enchanting town of Doncaster, South Yorkshire, England, her journey through life is a testament to resilience, devotion, and a determination to make a difference.

From her earliest days, Paris was nurtured within the embrace of her traditional gypsy heritage, imbibing values of family unity, loyalty, and the strength to weather life's storms. These values would become the guiding principles of her life's narrative.

Paris's destiny took a fateful turn when she crossed paths with Tyson Fury, a young boxer whose dreams were as big as his heart. Their first meeting at a friend's wedding and the serendipitous reconnection on Paris's 16th birthday ignited a love story that would capture hearts around the world. Their journey reached its pinnacle with a mesmerizing wedding ceremony in 2008, a celebration of their enduring bond witnessed by an assembly of loved ones.

As Tyson Fury's star blazed in the boxing arena, Paris stood as his unwavering rock, offering support and strength through triumphs and challenges alike. Amid raising their six children and cultivating a nurturing family environment, she found her voice on social media. With over a million followers on Instagram and a significant presence on Twitter, Paris used her platform to empower and uplift, sharing her journey with authenticity and grace.

In 2021, Paris's story gained new dimensions with the release of her book, "Love and Fury: The Magic and Mayhem of Life with Tyson." In this poignant memoir, she opened her heart to readers, providing an intimate glimpse into their relationship's complexities, joys, and unbreakable love.

Even in the face of adversity, such as the pain of two miscarriages, Paris's spirit remained unshakable. Her willingness to speak openly about these experiences resonated with countless individuals who found solace in her vulnerability and strength.

Paris Fury's life serves as a beacon of love and empowerment. Beyond being the wife of a boxing champion, she exemplifies authenticity, self-love, and resilience. Her legacy continues to inspire those navigating their own journeys, reminding us that true strength lies in embracing our individuality, facing challenges head-on, and leaving a lasting legacy of love, courage, and empowerment.

As Paris's journey unfolds, her story remains a testament to the transformative power of love and the lasting impact of empowering oneself and others. Through her example, she reminds us that life's most significant contributions are often found in the way we inspire, uplift, and champion the human spirit.

Printed in Great Britain
by Amazon

27465219R00020